M. Smith

A Guide for Using

The Magic School Bus® on the Ocean Floor

in the Classroom

Based on the book written by Joanna Cole

This guide written by Ruth M. Young, M.S. Ed.

Teacher Created Materials, Inc.
6421 Industry Way
Westminster, CA 92683
www.teachercreated.com

©*1996 Teacher Created Materials, Inc.*
Reprinted, 1999

Made in U.S.A.
ISBN 1-57690-085-1

Edited by
Mary Kaye Taggart

Illustrated by
José L. Tapia

Cover Art by
Wendy Chang & Diane Birnbaum

The classroom teacher may reproduce copies of materials in this book for classroom use only. The reproduction of any part for an entire school or school system is strictly prohibited. No part of this publication may be transmitted, stored, or recorded in any form without written permission from the publisher.

Table of Contents

Introduction

The use of trade books can enhance the study of science. The key to selecting these books is to check them for scientific accuracy and appropriateness for the level of the students. *The Magic School Bus*® series, written by Joanna Cole, is an outstanding example of books which can help students enjoy and learn about science. These books are delightfully written and scientifically accurate, thanks to the thorough research done by the author as she writes each of her books.

This *Science/Literature Unit* is directly related to *The Magic School Bus*® *on the Ocean Floor*. The activities in this unit are particularly appropriate for intermediate grades. Teachers who use this unit will find a variety of lessons to do before, during, and after reading the book with their students. These include the following:

- A Pre-reading Activity
- A Biographical Sketch and Picture of the Author
- A Book Summary
- Activity-oriented lessons which expand the topics covered in the story:
  — comparing the area of water to land on earth
  — observing live goldfish
  — comparing the density of fresh water and salt water
  — comparing the density of hot and cold water
  — plotting a tide graph for a month
  — creating a mural depicting views of the ocean floor
  — dissecting a fish
  — sorting and identifying plankton drawings
  — measuring the lengths of sharks
  — investigating life in the ocean's depths
  — making a model of the ocean floor
  — constructing a pop-up book of life on a reef

- A Post-reading Activity
- Unit Assessment
- Annotated List of Books and Materials
- Answer Key

This unit is designed to help you present exciting lessons for your students so that they can develop their understanding and appreciation of the earth's oceans.

The Magic School Bus® *is a registered trademark of Scholastic, Inc.*

What Do You Know?

Before reading *The Magic School Bus® on the Ocean Floor,* have the students make word webs which consist of words and/or phrases that come to their minds when they hear the word "ocean." Have your students work in groups of four or five to create their word webs. Instruct them to put their ideas on a map in a random order, as in the first example below. Then, make one large web by compiling the ideas from each group. When the information has been compiled, link the related ideas together, as shown in the second example below. Display the large word web in the classroom and ask your students to add new information throughout the unit.

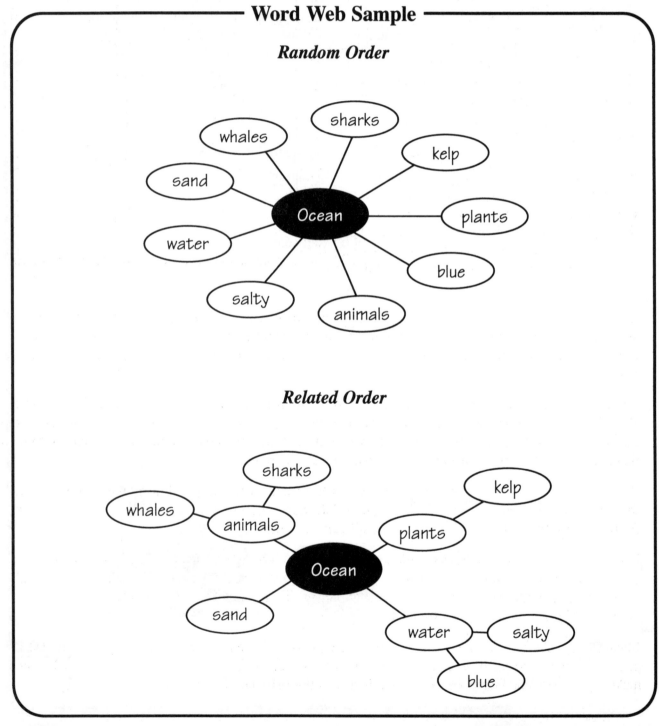

About the Author

Joanna Cole was born on August 11, 1944, in New York. She attended the University of Massachusetts and Indiana University before receiving her B.A. from the City College of the City University of New York in 1967. She worked as an elementary library teacher and letters correspondent at *Newsweek* and then became senior editor of books for young readers at Doubleday and Company.

Ms. Cole has written over 20 books for children, most of which are nonfiction. Every writer begins his/her career somewhere; Joanna Cole's began with cockroaches. While she was working as a library teacher in a Brooklyn elementary school, her father gave her an article about cockroaches and how they were on the earth before the dinosaurs. She had enjoyed reading science books as a child and remembered finding books about insects to be the most fascinating. Since there were not any books about cockroaches, she decided to write one. Her first book, *Cockroaches,* was published in 1971.

Cole has written about fleas, dinosaurs, chicks, fish, saber-toothed tigers, frogs, horses, hurricanes, snakes, cars, puppies, insects, and babies, just to name several examples. Ms. Cole knows that the important thing is to make the book so fascinating that the reader will be eager to go on to the next page.

Teachers and children have praised Ms. Cole's ability to make science interesting and understandable. Her Magic School Bus® series has now made science funny, as well. Joanna says that before she wrote this series, she had a goal to write good science books telling stories that would be so much fun to read that readers would read them even without the science component.

Readers across the country love the Magic School Bus® series and enjoy following the adventures of the wacky science teacher, Ms. Frizzle. Joanna Cole works closely with Bruce Degen, the illustrator for this series, to create fascinating and scientifically accurate books for children.

Even a successful writer finds it sometimes scary to begin writing a new book. That was the way Joanna felt before beginning to write the Magic School Bus® series. She says, "I couldn't work at all. I cleaned out closets, answered letters, went shopping— anything but sit down and write. But eventually I did it, even though I was scared."

Joanna Cole says kids often write their own Magic School Bus® adventures. She suggests they just pick a topic and a place for a field trip. Do a lot of research about the topic. Think of a story line and make it funny. Some kids even like to put;their own teachers into their stories.

The Magic School Bus®
on the Ocean Floor

by Joanna Cole

(Scholastic, 1987)

(Canada, Scholastic; UK, Scholastic Limited; AUS, Scholastic Party Limited)

Ms. Frizzle's class is studying the ocean, so she suggests that they go to the ocean the next day. All of the students are really excited; they think they are going to the beach. They are in for a real surprise! The next day, they pile into the old bus, which once again works its magic. It does not stop at the beach but drives right into the ocean. The bus even takes an unexpected passenger as it enters the water—Lenny, the lifeguard who is trying to save the students and Ms. Frizzle.

The Friz announces to all of her passengers that the best way to learn about the ocean is to see it up close. Beginning their adventure at the continental shelf, the entire group leaves the bus, dressed in diving gear complete with face masks and air tanks. They swim with a school of fish and look at the sea stars, clams, and other creatures in this shallow area. Ms. Frizzle has a microscope for them to use to examine the tiny plankton in the water.

Suddenly, they find themselves swimming with sharks! Ms. Frizzle assures them that most sharks do not eat humans. Then, she and some of the students hitch a ride on a whale shark. A whale shark is a shark, but it is so large that it is named after the largest sea animal, the whale.

The class and the bus dive deeper and deeper until the surroundings become very dark and cold and they feel the water pressure increase.

They climb inside the bus, which has changed into a deep diving submersible. Through the windows, they view the strange creatures which live at these depths, including fish which glow. They come upon a vent of hot lava, pushing up from beneath the earth's crust, which makes a vent in the ocean floor. It looks as if no life could exist here, but they are surprised to find tube worms eight to ten feet long! They also see colorless, blind crabs and shrimp and an animal which looks like a flower.

Next, the bus surfaces and becomes a glass-bottomed boat through which they can see a beautiful coral reef surrounding an island. Once again, they put on their diving outfits and go swimming to see the beautiful reef fish and coral.

The Friz calls everyone back aboard the bus, which transforms into a giant surfboard. They follow the ocean current and ride the waves, along with dolphins and a whale, back to the beach. All have their pictures taken with Lenny, who claims that he has saved them all.

Back at school, the students are so inspired that they create a map of the ocean, showing the fantastic things that they saw at each depth of the water. They also include the birds that they saw flying over the water. What a way to learn about the ocean!

How Big Is the Ocean?

Ms. Frizzle's students have been hard at work investigating various topics related to their study of the ocean, including environmental issues and animals found in the ocean. Wanda has written a report about how big the oceans are. She reports that "There is more water than land on earth."

Read the facts below to become familiar with the divisions on a globe. Then, use the Northern and Southern Hemisphere maps on pages 9 and 10 to compare the amount of land covered by the oceans and the amount of land above sea level.

Latitude and Longitude Facts:

The globe is divided by latitude and longitude lines to make it easier to find locations on the earth. *Latitude* lines are parallel circles beginning at the equator and moving north and south. The latitude of the equator is 0°, the North Pole is 90° north (90° N), and the South Pole is 90° south (90° S).

Longitude lines are half circles drawn from pole to pole. They are counted from the prime meridian, which goes through the original location of the Royal Observatory in Greenwich, England. These lines are measured east and west of the prime meridian. Latitude and longitude lines form a grid on a map.

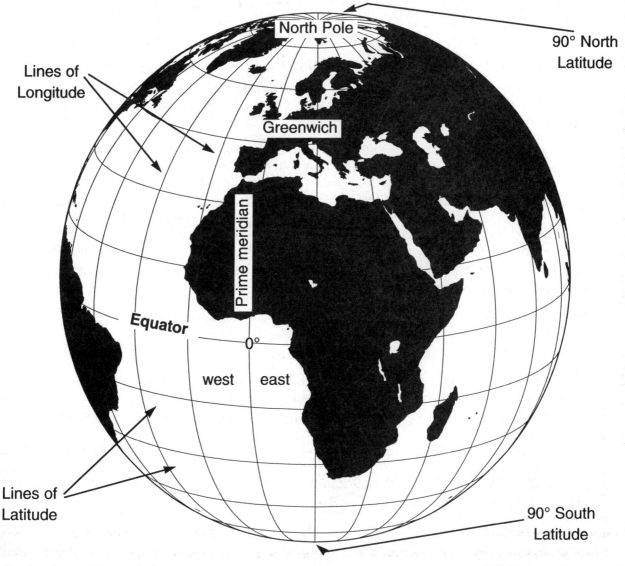

How Big Is the Ocean? *(cont.)*

Look at the Northern and Southern Hemisphere maps on pages 9 and 10 to complete the following information.

Find the latitude circles on the maps.

1. How many degrees apart are the latitude circles from each other? _____°

2. The 10° and 20° latitude circles have been marked for you. Continue to number the latitude circles up to 80° on both maps.

3. How many latitude sections are there from the equator to each pole? [　　] latitude sections

The longitude lines are also shown 10° apart. These are drawn from the equator to the poles on both maps. The equator is a circle, so it is 360°. Use this information to complete the following.

4. How many sections of longitude are on this map? ( ) longitude sections
   Explain how you got your answer. _____

There are the same number of latitude sections from the equator to each pole; they get smaller as they get closer to the poles. Both maps have the same number of sections. You will need to know how many total sections there are on both maps. Use the information you learned from the questions above in the formula below to find the total sections on both maps.

5. [　　] latitude sections x ( ) longitude sections = _____ total sections on one map

6. _____ total sections on one map x 2 = [　　] MT (total sections on both maps)

Count the number of sections in each latitude ring which are all ocean (white) and those which show very little land (black).

Record the data on the chart below to discover how much of the earth is covered by water. The first one has been done for you.

Amount of the Earth Covered by Water

Latitude Section	Northern Hemisphere	Southern Hemisphere
0° – 10°	30 sections	_____ sections
10° – 20°	_____ sections	_____ sections
20° – 30°	_____ sections	_____ sections
30° – 40°	_____ sections	_____ sections
40° – 50°	_____ sections	_____ sections
50° – 60°	_____ sections	_____ sections
60° – 70°	_____ sections	_____ sections
70° – 80°	_____ sections	_____ sections
80° – 90°	_____ sections	_____ sections
Totals:	[　　] (N) sections	( ) (S) sections

[　　] (N) + ( ) (S) = [　　] (T) Total sections covered by oceans

[　　] (T) ÷ [　　] (MT)* = _____ % of earth covered by oceans

*Total latitude and longitude sections on both maps from number 6.

How Big Is the Ocean? *(cont.)*

Northern Hemisphere

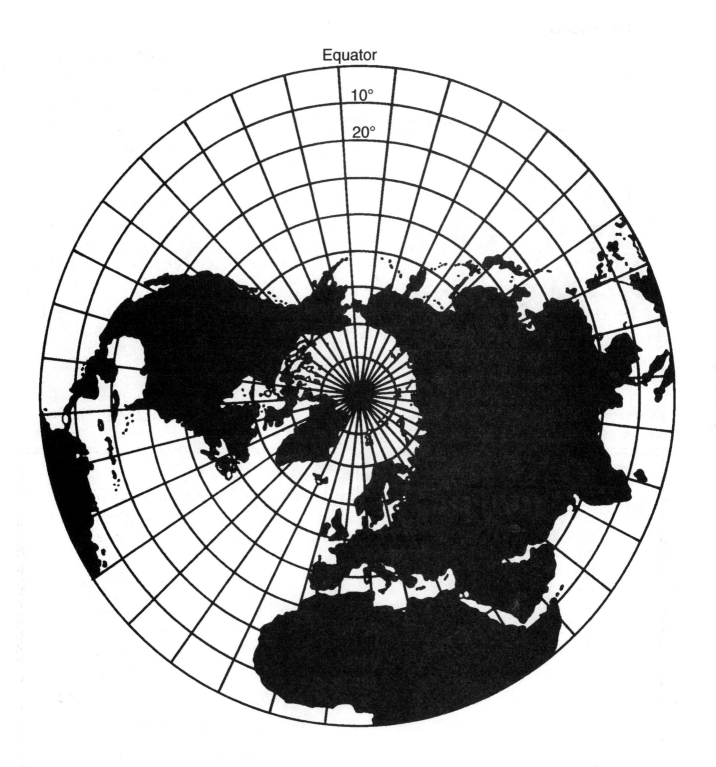

How Big Is the Ocean? *(cont.)*

Southern Hemisphere

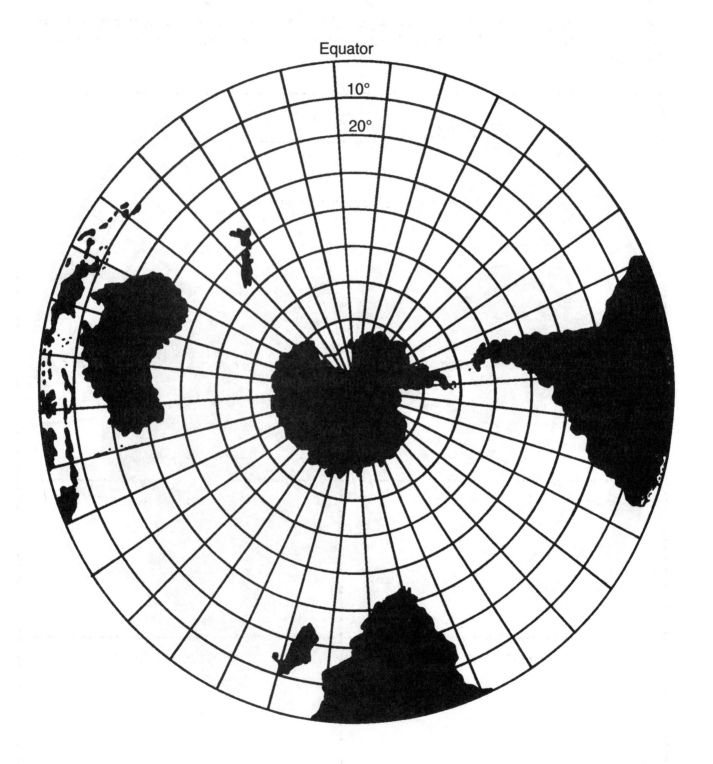

Gone Fishing

Ms. Frizzle's students made posters of some of the animals which live in the sea, including comparing how they move. Observe a live fish to see how much you can learn about it.

Materials: goldfish, guppy, or other small fish; fish bowl or large jar; a piece of gauze

Procedure: Gently place a fish into a bowl or jar. Place the gauze over the bowl so that the fish will not be able to jump out. (Hold the gauze in place with a rubber band.) Watch the fish as it swims for a few minutes.

Watching a _____
(type of fish)

Compare the way a fish swims with the way a person swims.

_____

_____

_____

Describe what your fish looks like and then make drawings of four different views of it. Add as much detail as you can. Label the parts of the fish. Use arrows to show the ways it moves its fins and body.

_____

_____

Side View	**Front View**
Rear View	**View from Above**

Comparing Salt Water to Fresh Water

Tim's report titled *Why Is the Ocean Salty?* stated that much of the salt in ocean water comes from the rocks which are worn down by water. Although ocean water tastes salty, it is really only about 3.5% salt. Most of the salt is sodium chloride, which is the salt we use to flavor our food. The amount of salt in the ocean is not the same everywhere. In areas where it is very warm, the surface water evaporates, and the water is saltier. Near the equator, it rains a lot, adding fresh water to the ocean surface. This makes the ocean so it is less salty here. Do an experiment to compare salt water and fresh water.

Materials: salt, water, green and blue food coloring, two droppers, two clear 1 oz. (30 mL) cups, two 9 oz. (270 mL) cups, green and blue crayons or markers, balance

Procedure: Pour tap water into the two 9 oz. (270 mL) cups until they are half full. Pour 1 tablespoon (15 mL) of salt into one of these containers and stir the water until the salt dissolves. Pour enough of this salt water into one of the 1 oz. cups to fill it ¾ full. Then, add drops of green food coloring to the small cup of salt water to make it dark green. Fill the other small cup ¾ full with fresh water and color it dark blue. Place a dropper in each of the small water cups.

Use the dropper to add drops of the green salt water to the clear fresh water. Observe and draw what happens. Add drops of the blue fresh water to the cup of clear salt water. Draw what you observe. Use the crayons to show the location of the salt water (green) and fresh water (blue) in your drawings.

Adding Salt Water to Fresh Water   Adding Fresh Water to Salt Water

9 oz. cup

9 oz. cup

Answer the following questions on a separate piece of paper.

1. What happened to the salt water when it was added to the fresh water?

2. What happened to the fresh water when it was added to the salt water?

3. Refill the small cups with green salt water and blue fresh water, putting the exact same amounts of water in each of them. Place them on different sides of a balance. What do you notice? How does this explain what happened in your experiment with the salt water and fresh water?

4. What do you think happens when fresh water runs into ocean water? Why?

Comparing Warm to Cold Water

Not all ocean water is the same temperature. Water near the Arctic and Antarctic areas is very cold, while water near the equator is warmer. Like salt water and fresh water, the density of cold and warm water is different. The density affects the way the water moves in the ocean. This experiment is like the one using salt water and fresh water, only this time the water will be hot and cold.

Materials: ice water, hot water, red and blue food coloring, two droppers, one clear 9 oz. (270 mL) cup, two clear 1 oz. (30 mL) cups, red and blue crayons or markers

Procedure: Fill the large cup ³/₄ full with the tap water and let it sit so that it becomes the temperature of the room. Pour hot water into one 1 oz. (30 mL) cup and cold water into the other until each cup is half full. Add drops of red food coloring to the hot water to make it dark red. Stir some drops of blue food coloring into the cold water until it becomes dark blue. Place a dropper in each of the small cups. Try to keep both cups of water either hot or cold.

Use the dropper to add drops of the hot water (red) to the water in the large cup. Do not empty the large cup, but add drops of the cold water (blue) to it. Repeat this experiment and draw what happens. Use the crayons to show the location of the hot (red) and cold (blue) water in your drawings.

Hot Water Added

9 oz. cup

(same cup of room temperature water)

Cold Water Added

9 oz. cup

1. What happens when the hot water is added?

   _____

   _____

2. What happens when the cold water is added?

   _____

   _____

3. What do you think happens when cold water from the Arctic or Antarctic Ocean meets warmer ocean water?

   _____

   _____

What Causes the Tides?

The children in Ms. Frizzle's class came dressed to spend the day at the beach. However, when the bus arrived at the beach the Friz drove right into the ocean! They drove into the intertidal zone, which is the area on the beach that experiences high and low tides. Rachel reported that the "tides are caused mostly by the pull of the moon's gravity on the earth and its oceans." How do you think scientists know this? Plot the rise and fall of the tide each day for one month to see this relationship. This activity uses the tide data collected for San Diego, California, in February of 1996.

Materials: 29 copies of the tide graph on page 18, a copy of the tide table on page 17 for each student, clear tape, black felt pens

Procedure: Date each of the 29 tide graphs from February 1 through February 29, 1996. Assign each student (or set of partners) a date from the Tide Table to plot on a Tide Graph. Ask them to use pencils to plot the data and connect the dots with curved lines. Then, have them trace over the dots and curved line with black pens. Tell them not to extend the lines beyond the first and last dots of data. Shown below is an example of how to plot the tide for February 1.

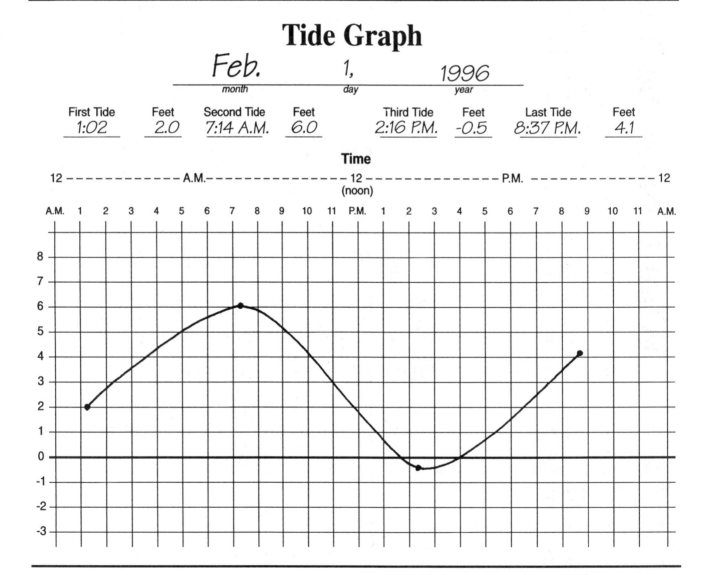

What Causes the Tides? *(cont.)*

Procedure *(cont.)*: After all of the 29 tide graphs have been completed, put the graphs in order by date. Fold each graph along the midnight line on the right side. Lay the graph for February 1 under the February 2 graph so that the midnight lines are on top of each other and then tape them in place. Continue adding each day's graph to the next in consecutive order. When all 29 graphs have been taped together, use a felt pen to connect the dates so that the curved line connects across the graphs. See the example below.

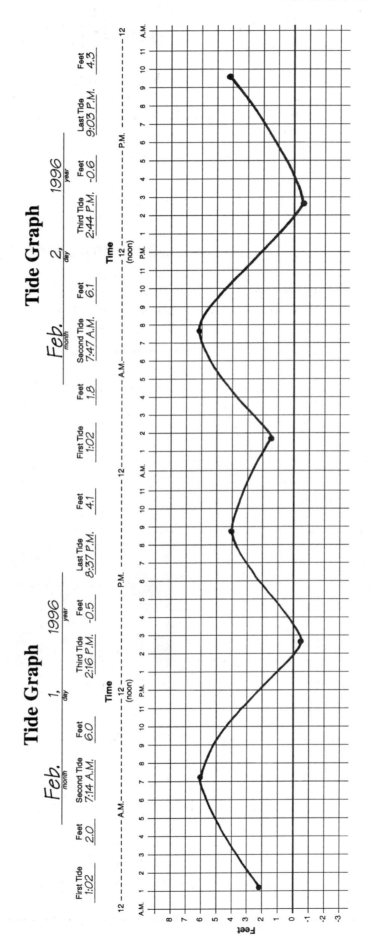

What Causes the Tides? *(cont.)*

Closure: Pin the tide graphs to the bulletin board and look at them to see what happens to the tides throughout the month.

Answer the questions below to help you analyze this data.

1. Does the tide rise and fall to the same levels every day? _____

2. Circle the dates when the tides are extremely high and extremely low:

    1   2   3   4   5   6   7   8   9   10

    11   12   13   14   15   16   17   18   19   20

    21   22   23   24   25   26   27   28   29

3. Circle the dates when the tides show very little change between high and low:

    1   2   3   4   5   6   7   8   9   10

    11   12   13   14   15   16   17   18   19   20

    21   22   23   24   25   26   27   28   29

4. If one of the four moon phases below happens to represent the day you graphed, cut it out and tape it on your tide graph.

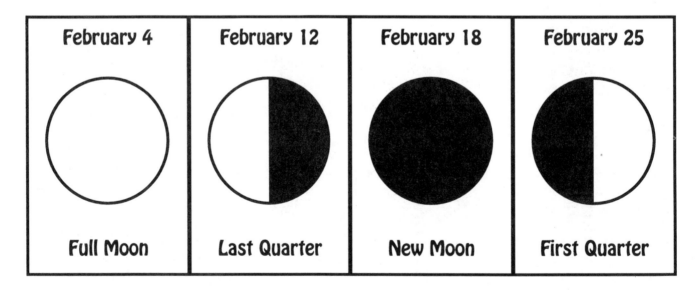

| February 4 | February 12 | February 18 | February 25 |
| Full Moon | Last Quarter | New Moon | First Quarter |

5. Compare the dates of the moon phases with the dates you circled above. What proof do you see that the moon's phases are related to the rising and falling of the tides?

_____

_____

6. Look at the diagram of the moon's phases on page 21 and the diagrams of the Explanation of the Tides on pages 19 and 20 to get more information on how the moon causes the tides.

Tide Table

Use the following tide table to plot a graph for your assigned day from February 1996. Place a ruler or straight edge below the information for the date you will be plotting to help you focus on only the information pertinent to you. Then, copy the data for your date to the top of your tide graph before plotting the graph.

Tide Table
San Diego, California
February 1996

Date	First Tide A.M.	Feet	Second Tide A.M. (except as noted)	Feet	Third Tide P.M.	Feet	Last Tide P.M.	Feet
1	1:02	2.0	7:14	6.0	2:16	-0.5	8:37	4.1
2	1:38	1.8	7:47	6.1	2:44	-0.6	9:03	4.3
3	2:10	1.6	8:18	6.2	3:10	-0.7	9:28	4.4
4	2:41	1.5	8:47	6.1	3:36	-0.6	9:52	4.5
5	3:13	1.4	9:17	6.0	4:01	-0.5	10:18	4.6
6	3:45	1.4	9:47	5.7	4:26	-0.2	10:45	4.7
7	4:21	1.4	10:20	5.3	4:52	0.1	11:14	4.8
8	5:02	1.4	10:56	4.9	5:20	0.4	11:48	4.8
9	5:51	1.5	11:39	4.3	5:52	0.9	next day	—
10	12:29	4.9	6:57	1.5	12:39	3.6	6:31	1.4
11	1:23	4.9	8:27	1.4	2:14	3.1	7:29	1.8
12	2:34	5.1	10:08	1.0	4:23	3.1	8:58	2.2
13	3:53	5.4	11:26	0.3	5:54	3.4	10:33	2.1
14	5:04	5.8	12:23 P.M.	-0.4	6:50	3.9	11:46	1.8
15	6:05	6.4	1:10 P.M.	-1.0	7:33	4.4	next day	—
16	12:44	1.4	6:57	6.8	1:53	-1.4	8:12	4.9
17	1:35	0.9	7:46	7.0	2:33	-1.6	8:50	5.3
18	2:23	0.5	8:32	7.0	3:11	-1.5	9:27	5.6
19	3:09	0.3	9:16	6.8	3:48	-1.2	10:04	5.7
20	3:55	0.2	10:00	6.3	4:24	-0.8	10:41	5.7
21	4:42	0.3	10:44	5.6	4:59	-0.2	11:19	5.6
22	5:32	0.5	11:31	4.8	5:35	0.5	next day	—
23	12:00	5.4	6:28	0.8	12:24	4.0	6:11	1.2
24	12:46	5.1	7:39	1.1	1:36	3.3	6:34	1.8
25	1:43	4.8	9:12	1.2	3:32	3.0	7:59	2.3
26	2:59	4.6	10:47	1.0	5:36	3.1	9:44	2.6
27	4:20	4.7	11:54	0.6	6:38	3.4	11:13	2.5
28	5:25	4.9	12:40 P.M.	0.3	7:14	3.8	next day	—
29	12:09	2.2	6:14	5.2	1:15	0.0	7:41	4.1

Note: "Next day" means that the tide appeared early the next morning; thus th,ere were only three tide changes on this date.

Tide Graph

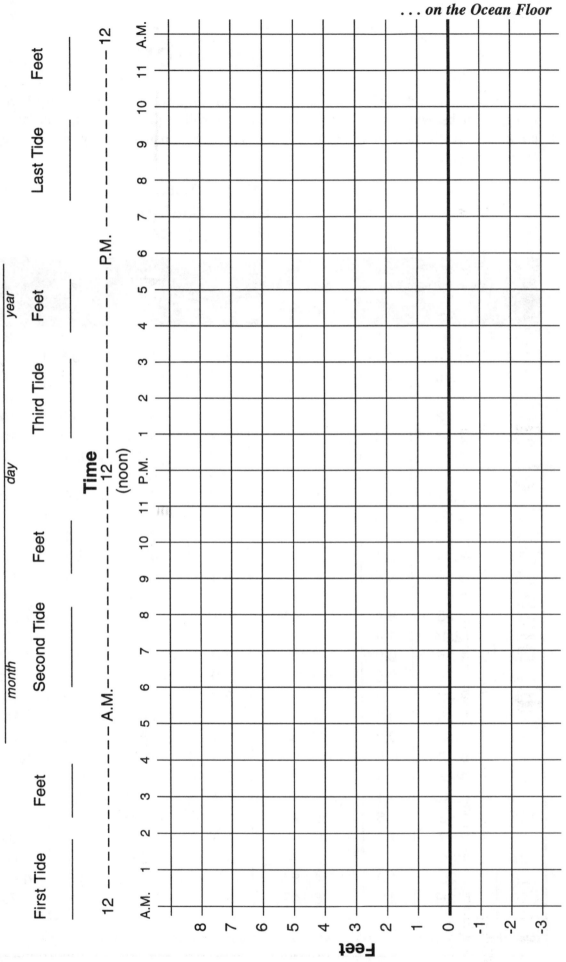

... on the Ocean Floor

Explanation of the Tides

Tides are mostly caused by the gravitational pull of the moon on the earth. The moon pulls the water directly below it, creating a high tide at that location. The opposite side of the earth also has a high tide since the moon pulls the solid earth away from the water on that side. Low tides occur between the high tides. As the earth rotates, different areas of the earth experience high and low tides about six hours apart.

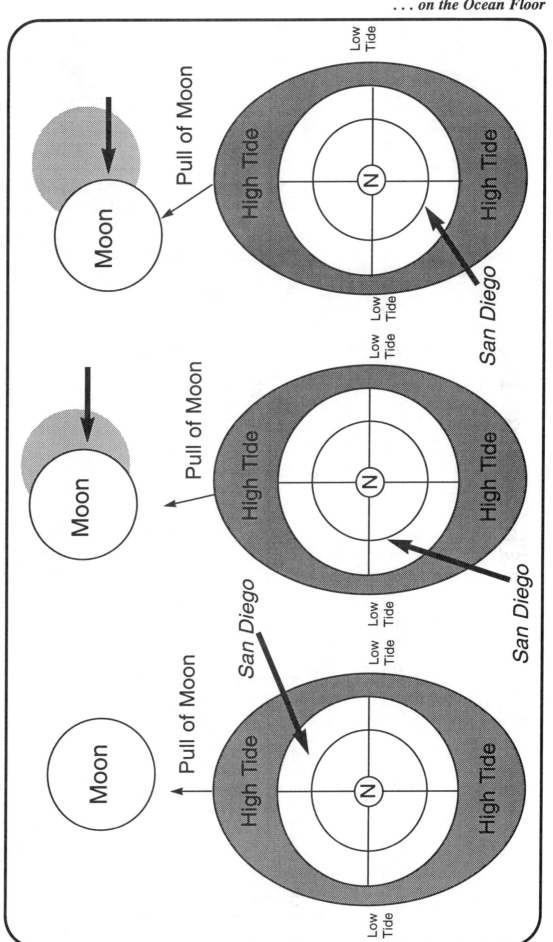

Explanation of the Tides *(cont.)*

Spring Tides

Spring tides are extremely high and extremely low. They occur when the moon and sun pull together on the earth. These tides occur when the moon is in the full or new phase.

Neap Tides

Neap tides generally occur when the moon is in its first or last quarter phase. The sun and moon pull at right angles to each other. This causes tides which are moderately low and high.

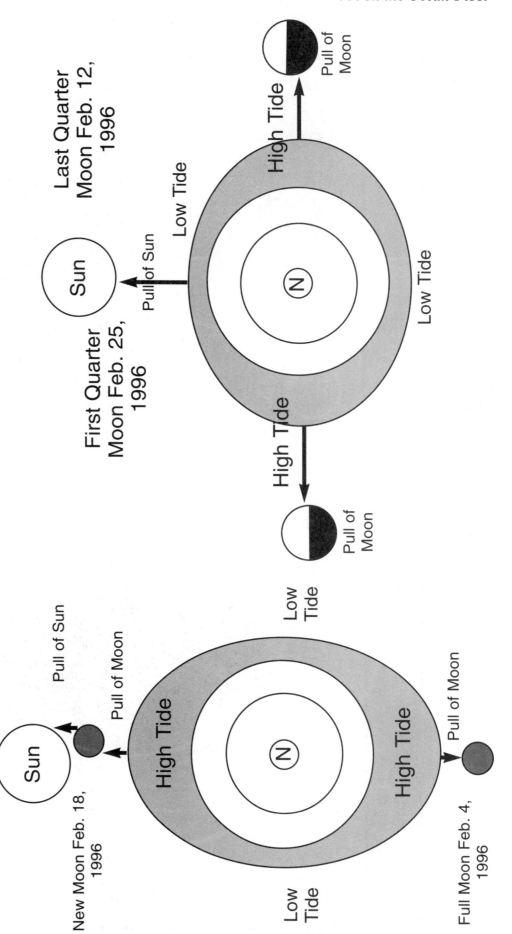

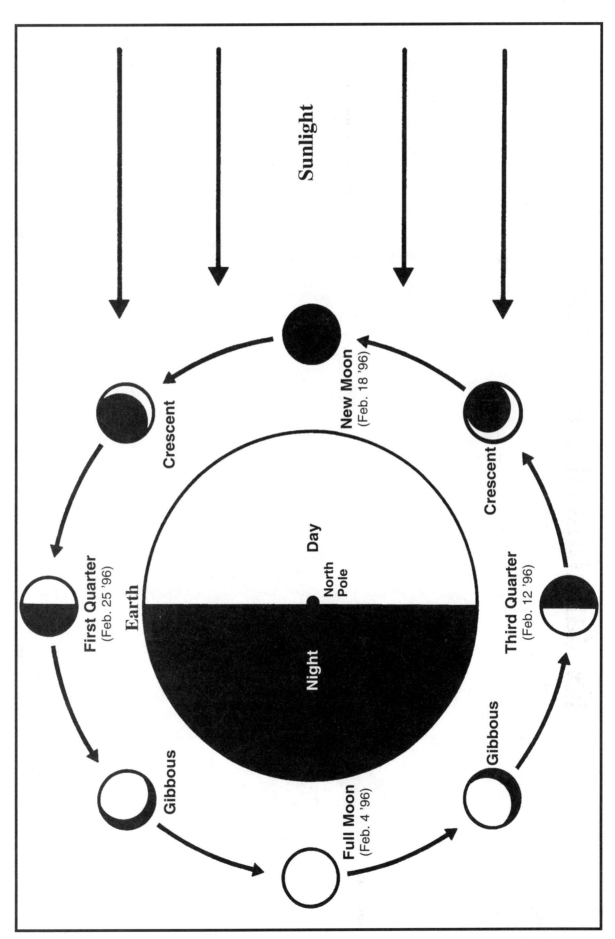

The Moon's Phases

Continental Shelf

As the bus drives into the ocean, it takes on a nautical appearance and drives along the continental shelf. Carmen's report said this was an edge around the continents which gradually slants down and is covered by water. The continental shelf varies in the distance it extends from the continents. Look at a map of the earth which shows the ocean floor, and you will see that the continental shelf of North America sticks out much further from the eastern coast than the western coast.

The continents are continually shifting. They are being moved by molten material seeping through the ocean floor from below the earth's crust. This process forms great ridges which run down the middle of the Atlantic Ocean floor and in areas of the Indian Ocean. As new material is added between the continents, parts of the earth's crust are being forced beneath other sections of the crust. This happens along the west coast of North America, causing earthquakes and pushing up mountains. (See page 46 for map information.)

This would be a good time to begin a picture record of the magic school bus' trip along the ocean floor. A large mural, consisting of pictures of things Ms. Frizzle's students see as they travel, makes a wonderful record. Pictures can gradually be added as each of the ocean topics is studied. When finished, it will show the continental shelf, continental slope, and the deepest part of the ocean.

Materials: 2 feet x 3 feet (60 cm x 90 cm) piece of blue butcher paper, colored felt pens or crayons, colored paper, glue, scissors

Procedure: Make a drawing of the bus and the passengers to glue onto the mural. Sketch in the plants and ocean floor. Use the book to get some ideas of the sea life found on the continental shelf, such as flounder, sea anemone, and squid. Look for pictures in other books about the ocean to add other sea life which might appear at this shallow area. Draw and color the pictures directly onto the mural or make them on other paper and paste them on. You may even want to glue on some real sea shells and sand. Be sure to add a title at the top of this section so that everyone will know it is the continental shelf.

Closure: Mount the mural near the ceiling. Additional sections may be added below it as your students study the continental slope and the deep ocean floor. Show that the continental shelf begins at the shoreline and continues to a depth of about 430 feet (131 m).

Its width averages 47 miles (75 km) but varies from 1 mile (1.6 km) along the Pacific coastline to 750 miles (1200 km) at the Arctic region.

Write a description of the continental shelf and the ocean scene shown in this section of the mural and place it near the picture.

Dissecting a Fish

It is time for all of the passengers on the bus to put on diving gear and swim along the continental shelf area. Here they discover lobsters, crabs, and schools of fish. Amanda Jane's report explains that fish breathe through their gills, rather than using lungs as people do.

Find out what a fish looks like close up. First, we look at the outside of a fish and then examine the inside.

Materials: a large fish which has not been cut open (may be purchased at a bait store), magnifying glass or microscope

Procedure: Begin by examining the outside of the fish. Use the drawing below to help you find these parts on your fish. Then, follow the directions on the next page.

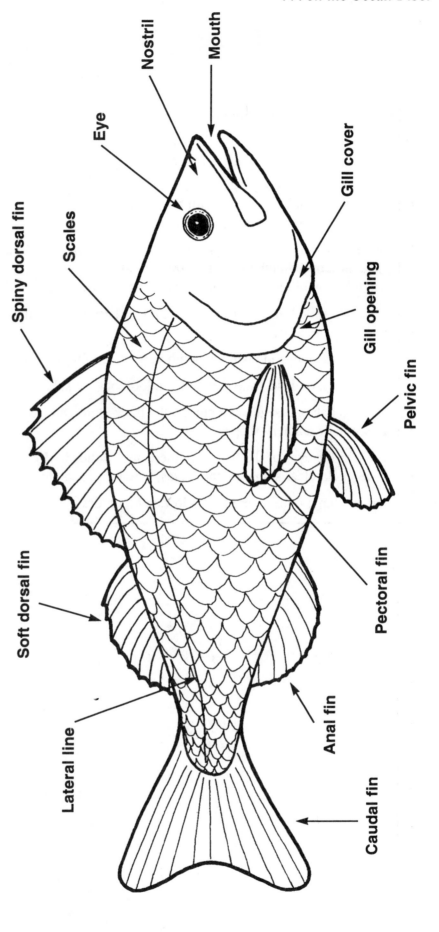

Dissecting a Fish *(cont.)*

Procedure *(cont.)*:

Follow these directions to continue examining the outside of the fish.

1. Look at the skin of the fish and notice that it is covered with overlapping scales. Pull out one of these scales and examine it with a magnifying glass or a microscope. Draw a picture of the scale.

   Scales show a series of rings, which are like growth rings of a tree. Ichthyologists, people who study fish, can tell how old a fish is from these rings.

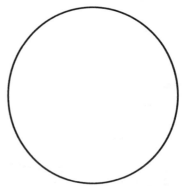

Magnified View of a Fish Scale

2. Find two little holes in front of the eyes. These are nostrils which are used by the fish to smell but not to breathe.

3. Pick up the fish and open its mouth very wide with the tweezers. Look for teeth and a tongue.

4. Open the mouth so wide that you can look out the side of the head. Can you see the gills?

5. Lay the fish on its side and pull up the thick skin which covers the gills. Look closely at the gills to see their feathery shape.

6. Look at the eyes of the fish. Are there any eyelids? Most fish do not have eyelids, but they do have thick, clear skin over their eyes, which protects them.

7. Draw a large outline of a fish below and then draw what you think is inside of the fish.

Dissecting a Fish *(cont.)*

Compare the drawing you just finished with the picture of the inside of a perch, shown on page 26. What organ is missing? After you are familiar with the organs inside a fish, follow the directions for dissection. You will see more if you do this slowly and carefully.

Materials: a large fish, sharp scissors, newspaper, drawing of the inside of a perch (page 26)

Procedure: Lay the fish on the newspaper and cut away the gill covering on one side. Cut out the gills so that you can see how feathery they are. They are usually red because there are blood vessels close to the surface of the skin so oxygen can be absorbed from the water as it passes over their gills.

Remove one eye by first cutting around the clear skin (cornea) and removing it. If you are careful, you should be able to probe under the eye with your scissors to lift it above the socket. Can you find the optic nerve which attaches to the back of the eye? Snip it so you can remove the eye. Look at the shape of the eye. It is flatter than your eyeball. Inside the eye is a lens; you should be able to find it if you carefully cut the eye open. The lens will look like a tiny, colorless ball. The colored part of the eye is the iris. It circles the opening into the eye, or the pupil. It may be difficult to find all of these parts if your fish is very small.

Locate the anus opening near the tail. Carefully put the point of the scissors into this opening and cut along the belly towards the mouth. Try not to cut too deeply so that you do not damage the internal organs. Cut through the tough bone near the gills. Now, begin cutting along the lateral line which runs along the backbone. Stop cutting just above the cut where you first began to open the fish. Cut down to the anal opening. Next, you need to remove the long flap of skin you have just outlined with your scissors. Lift the edge  of the skin flap near the tail and gently pull on it as you cut away the muscle tissue underneath it with your scissors. Soon, you will see the cavity in which all the internal organs are located (as shown in the drawing). Carefully remove the entire flap of skin so that you can look at the organs. Do not disturb the organs but compare them to the drawing to identify them.

Now, look for the heart; it is small and triangularly shaped. Just as your heart and lungs are close together, the fish heart is near the gills, which are its lungs. Blood is pumped from the heart through the gills to exchange carbon dioxide for oxygen from the water. Next, the blood enters the dorsal aorta. It is then distributed throughout the body and back to the heart. This circulation pattern is repeated all during the life of the fish.

Look for the clear balloon of skin near the backbone. This is an air bladder which the fish uses to help it move up and down in the water. Can you find the stomach? Cut it open to see what the fish had for its last meal. Try to find some of the other organs which are shown in the drawing, such as the intestines. If this is a female fish, you may find the ovary with eggs in it.

Closure: Write a letter to someone to tell what you learned about this fish. Be sure to make drawings of the outside and inside of the fish to go along with the letter. Label the parts of your drawing so that the reader will be able to know what the parts of the fish are.

Inside a Perch

Carefully follow the directions on the previous page as you dissect your fish. Use the diagram below to identify the parts of the perch.

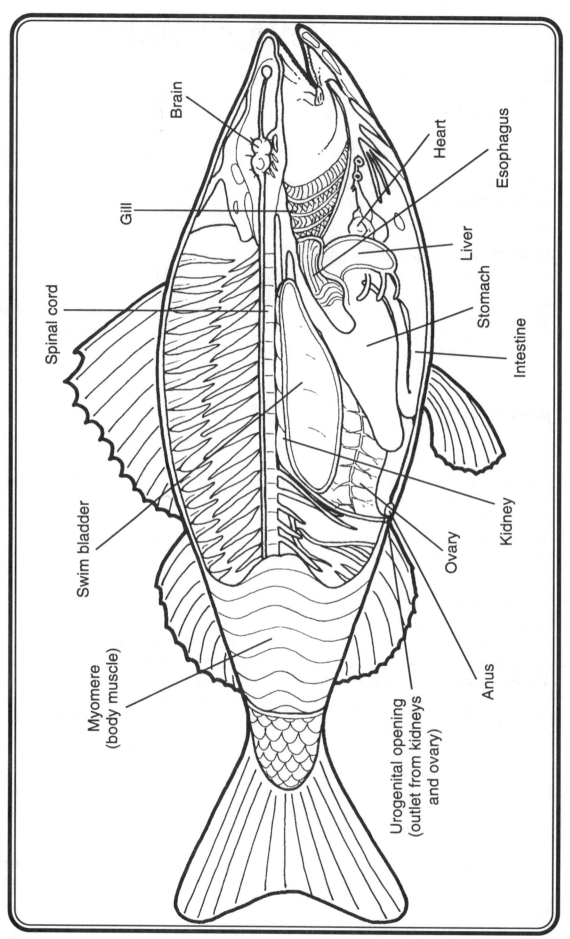

Brain

Gill

Heart

Esophagus

Liver

Stomach

Intestine

Spinal cord

Swim bladder

Kidney

Ovary

Anus

Myomere (body muscle)

Urogenital opening (outlet from kidneys and ovary)

© *Teacher Created Materials, Inc.*

Sorting Plankton

Ms. Frizzle, always prepared, has brought along a microscope so that her students can look at the tiny plankton swimming in the ocean. The boys and girls are fascinated as they look at the phytoplankton (plant) and zooplankton (animal) specimens. They even see plankton eating plankton! John's report says that "plankton plants make food by using energy from the sun," just as other plants on our planet do. Also, they give off much of the oxygen which is released into the water and atmosphere.

John's report also describes the food chain in the ocean, which begins with plankton eating other plankton. These are eaten by larger animals, which are eaten by even bigger animals, and the chain of food continues. All of this would be impossible if the sun did not give energy to the phytoplankton.

Materials: a set of 16 plankton specimens for each group, transparency copies of pages 28 and 29, 2 feet x 3 feet (60 cm x 90 cm) blue butcher paper, crayons, felt pens

Procedure: The object of this activity is to have the students determine whether the plankton specimens are plant or animal, based upon their previous knowledge of the characteristics of plants and animals. Make enlarged copies of the 16 pictures of plankton specimens from pages 28 and 29. Cut them into sets for the students, removing the identification letters. Make a transparency of each page, as well. Divide the students into groups of three or four and give each group a set of the 16 plankton specimens. Tell them that plankton are either plant or animal. Challenge the students to sort their plankton specimens into those two categories, based upon the features shown in the pictures. Discuss the features used by students to sort the plankton. Let them walk around the room and look at the different ways other groups sorted the same specimens.

Closure: Show the transparency of the phytoplankton and zooplankton and have students compare these to the way they sorted their specimens. Let them correct their group's plankton specimens. Discuss the specimens which were difficult to identify and let the students show the characteristics these specimens have or lack that caused them to be misidentified. Point out the variations in the sizes of plankton, especially the jellyfish, which can be as large as 98 feet (30 m) and as small as the tiny diatoms (.0032 inches/15 μm).

Extender: Add the continental slope section to the ocean mural. Use another 2 feet (60 cm) of blue butcher paper. Make drawings of various plankton specimens. Glue these to the mural. Design a series of small to large sea animals to show a food chain and place them on the mural. Add a title to this section and describe that it plunges to depths of 2.75 miles (4.4 km) below the continental shelf. The slope forms the sides of the continents, and its width ranges from 12 to 60 miles (20 to 100 km).

Mount this section of the ocean mural on the wall beneath the continental shelf section. Write a brief description of the sea life at this depth and display it near this section.

Zooplankton

Animal Plankton

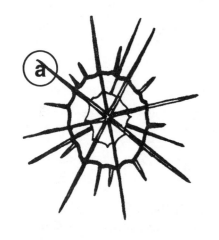

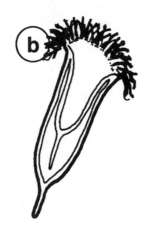

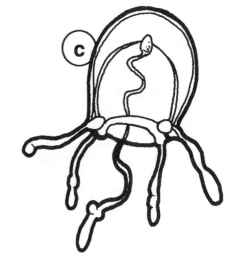

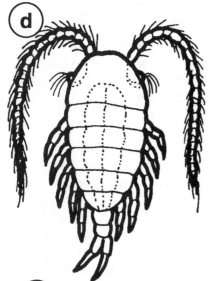

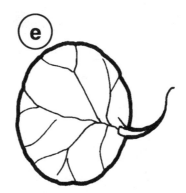

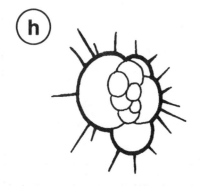

Zooplankton Key

Name	Largest Size
a. radiolaria	.02 in. (.5 mm)
b. tintinnid	.002 in. (50 μm)
c. jellyfish	98 ft. (30 m)
d. copepod	0.2 in. (5 mm)
e. dinoflagellate	.04 in. (1 mm)
f. jellyfish	98 ft. (30 m)
g. fish larva	2 in. (5 cm)
h. foraminifera	.04 in. (1 mm)

μm=micro millimeter; 1 mm=1000 μm

Phytoplankton

Plant Plankton

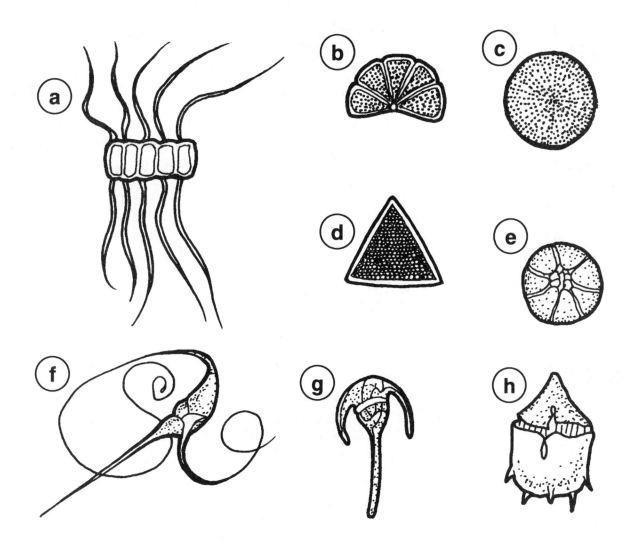

Phytoplankton Key

Diatoms	**Largest Size**
a–e	.0032 in. (15 µm)
Dinoflagellates	**Largest Size**
f–h	.004 in. (100 µm)

µm=micro millimeter; 1 mm=1000 µm

Sharks: Friend or Foe

The next sea life Ms. Frizzle and her students meet are sharks! Ms. Frizzle tells them not to worry, since most sharks do not eat people. The children panic anyway. Should they be afraid of all sharks?

Ask your students to write about their knowledge of sharks in this next activity. They will brainstorm what they already know on this subject and write these words in a word web format as described on page four. Challenge your students to then read reference books about sharks to learn more. Following their reading and discussion, they will make another word web to show what they have learned.

Materials: large pieces of white paper, black felt pens

Procedure: Read the information about sharks provided by Ms. Frizzle and her students in the book. Ask each of the students to write a list of three things which they already know about sharks.

Divide the students into groups of three or four. Instruct the groups to write these ideas in the word web format on large pieces of paper. The unfinished example below may help students begin their webs.

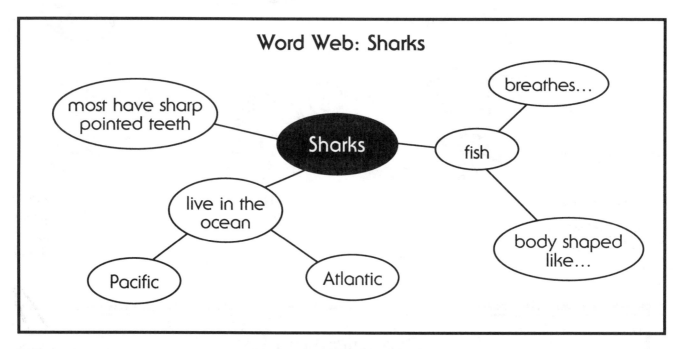

Display the webs in the classroom and let a spokesperson from each group tell about their web. Provide many books and other references about sharks for each group to expand their knowledge of sharks. After each group has had time to research the topic of sharks, have them make a second web and compare it with their earlier one. Compile this information and make one large word web about sharks to display with the web made about the ocean earlier in this unit.

Extender: Let each group choose a different species of shark to draw, color, and add to the continental slope section of the ocean mural. Ask the students to draw their sharks to the same scale so that the viewer can get a feel for the different sizes of sharks. The pictures of the sharks in the next activity will provide examples for the students to use.

How Big Are Sharks?

Sharks have been on the earth for more than 400 million years, and they appeared long before any animals walked on land. There are more than 350 species (types) of sharks. They range in size from the tiny spined pygmy, which grows to be 10 inches (25 cm), to the huge whale shark that can become 50 feet long (15 meters). Do the following activity to demonstrate the size range of seven types of sharks.

Materials: 140 feet (42 meters) of string, pictures of sharks mounted on cardboard, yardstick or meterstick, hole punch

Procedure: Enlarge the pictures of the sharks shown below and on the next page. Cut out the sharks and mount each of them on cardboard. Divide the students into seven groups and give each a shark. Ask the students to gather information about their sharks, including the information given with the pictures. Then, have the students write all of the collected information on the backs of the shark pictures. Punch a hole in a corner of each picture. Instruct the groups to measure pieces of string the same length as their sharks and tie the strings to their shark pictures. Tie knots in the other ends of the strings so that they will not fray. As a class, take the shark cards outside and stretch out the strings, beginning at the same point so that the lengths can be compared.

Sharks!

Great White 21 feet (6.4 m)

The white sharks are the world's largest predatory fish. They are mostly found in cool waters.

Nurse 14 feet (4.3 m)

Unlike most sharks, nurse sharks do not have to swim continuously to breathe. They use special muscles to pump water over their gills. This allows them to rest and breathe at the same time.

Short Fin Mako 12 feet (3.7 m)

Makos are streamlined and built for speed. They are the fastest of the sharks with a swimming speed of up to 22 miles (35 km) per hour.

Scalloped Hammerhead 14 feet (4.3 m)

Hammerheads have an eye and a nostril at each end of their heads. Scientists think that this helps them to steer and find prey more easily. They sometimes form schools of up to 100 sharks.

How Big Are Sharks? *(cont.)*

Whale Shark 50 feet (15 m)

Whale sharks, which are the largest of the sharks, are not whales but are so big that they are sometimes mistaken for them. They can weigh more than 4000 pounds (1,800 kg) each. These giants are usually gentle creatures who eat plankton or fish no larger than a minnow. They have hundreds of tiny teeth in their jaws but have never been seen biting anything.

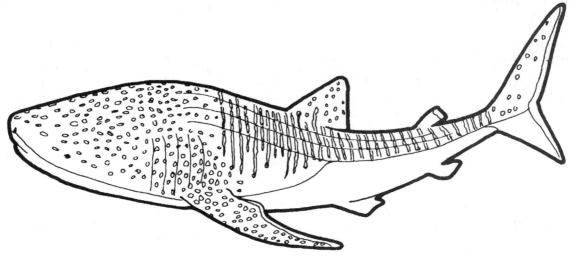

Thresher 20 feet (6.1 m)

Threshers use their long, powerful tails to herd schools of anchovies (fish) into tight balls. They sweep their tails through these balls, stunning and killing the fish.

Spined Pygmy 10 in. (25 cm)

The pygmy sharks are the smallest of the sharks. They live in the cold, dark, deep parts of the sea. They produce their own lights like lightning bugs do on the land. These lights are used to attract or find prey or mates.

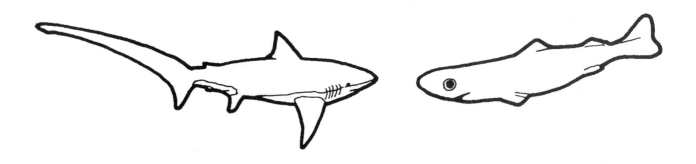

Extender: Make a transparency of the shark pictures and use an overhead projector to enlarge the images to their actual lengths on a long wall. This may be a real challenge for the whale shark!

The Bottom of the Ocean

After the adventure of riding on the whale shark, the students and Ms. Frizzle find their bus has been changed into a *submersible,* a deep-sea diving vessel. When they are inside of it, they are safe from the tremendous pressure of the weight of the water at this depth (which could crush them otherwise). Sunlight cannot shine this deeply into the water, so there are no plants. The students see some very strange looking fish that make their own light. The system used to make this light is like that used by fireflies and glowworms on land, and it is called bioluminescence. Shirley's report said that these "deep -sea animals often eat bits of food that sink from the upper ocean" to the bottom, or they attract food with their light, like the angler fish.

Some of the strangest and least known fish live at these great depths. Many have large eyes, huge mouths, and fang-like teeth, as well as light organs that flash on and off in the dark waters. This light may help them find each other in the dark. Most of these fish do not come to the surface, except the oarfish, which sometimes swims up from the lower midwaters. The oarfish looks a lot like a sea serpent as it breaks the surface and may have been mistaken for some kind of monster by early sailors.

The most surprising discovery was made in 1977 when life was discovered around warm water vents (called hydrothermal vents) in the Galapagos Rift on the ocean floor. The water is warmed when it makes contact with magma just below the crust. Deep-diving submersibles have discovered hundreds of large clams and mussels at depths as deep as 4 miles (6.4 km). Another study found vents with spaghetti-like acorn worms and tube worms 8 feet (2.4 m) long.

To the Student: As a class, design the last part of the ocean mural, showing the deepest part of the ocean.

Materials: 2 feet x 3 feet (60 cm x 90 cm) of black butcher paper; yellow, green, and blue paint

Procedure: Make pictures of some of the fish found at this depth, using the pictures on page 34 as well as those you can find in reference books about the ocean. Draw them in pencil, on black paper to show only their outlines and then add yellow, green, or blue paint to those fish which glow (i.e., lantern fish).

Add a hydrothermal vent at the bottom of the mural (see page 35). Use some creativity to make this area as realistic as possible. For example, cotton could represent the hot water rising from the vent. Long flexible tubes could be painted to look like the tube worms. String could be used to represent the spaghetti worms. Be sure to include a picture of the submersible magic school bus.

Closure: Make a sign for this section of the mural which reads "Deep Ocean Floor." Write a brief description of the strange animals which live there. Show that the depth may be as much as 6.5 miles (10.4 km).

Deep-Sea Fish

The creatures below live in the deepest part of the ocean. Use these illustrations as a guide in your drawing and research activity for the ocean mural. The given measurements are the average lengths of the fish.

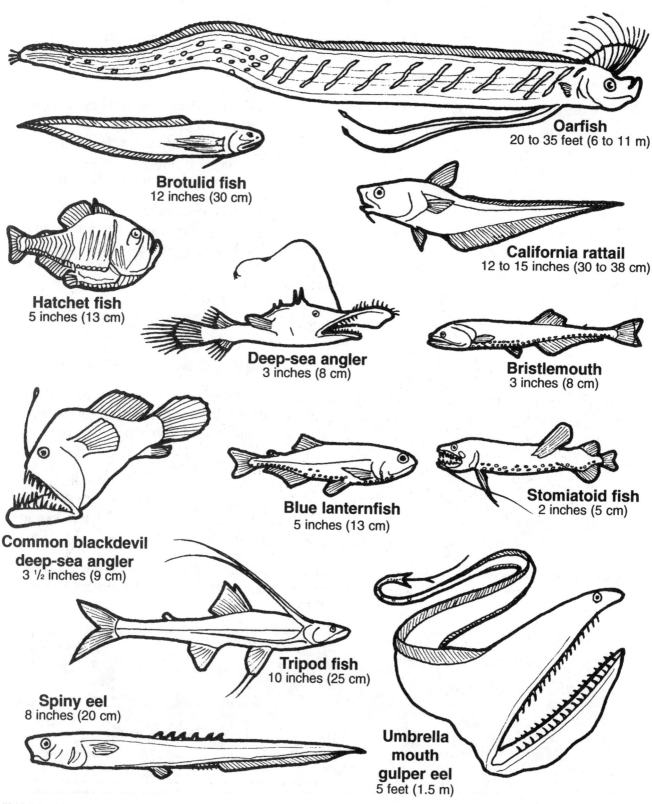

Oarfish
20 to 35 feet (6 to 11 m)

Brotulid fish
12 inches (30 cm)

California rattail
12 to 15 inches (30 to 38 cm)

Hatchet fish
5 inches (13 cm)

Deep-sea angler
3 inches (8 cm)

Bristlemouth
3 inches (8 cm)

Blue lanternfish
5 inches (13 cm)

Stomiatoid fish
2 inches (5 cm)

**Common blackdevil
deep-sea angler**
3 ½ inches (9 cm)

Tripod fish
10 inches (25 cm)

Spiny eel
8 inches (20 cm)

**Umbrella
mouth
gulper eel**
5 feet (1.5 m)

Hydrothermal Vent

Location: East Pacific Rise south of Baja, California

Below is an artist's version of what you might see if you were to take a voyage in a submersible. Use this illustration to help create the final section of the ocean mural.

Key

A. **Alvin**—submersible which can carry three passengers

B. **Blue lanternfish**

C. **Zoarcid fish**

D. **Hydrothermal vent**

E. **Tube worms**

F. **Sea stars**—colorless

G. **Crabs**—blind and colorless

H. **Clams**—huge and colorless

Deep as the Ocean

Ms. Frizzle has shown us that the depth of the ocean varies. In some areas, such as the continental shelf, it is shallow. However, the deepest trenches are up to 7 miles (11.3 km) below the surface of the water. How do scientists know this?

Long ago, the depths of shorelines were measured by sailors using ropes with weights on them. Units of measurement were marked off on these ropes. Sailors would lower a rope into the ocean and count the marks on it to find the depth. Today, we use sonar, which sends sound waves to the bottom of the ocean and records the time it takes for the sound waves to travel back to the surface. Using this data, scientists can map the ocean floor, showing ridges (mountains) and trenches (valleys). Satellite images are also now being used to provide more information about the shape of the ocean floor.

Do a simulation of mapping the ocean floor, using shoe boxes to represent the ocean. Ask your students to pretend that they are members of a scientific team which has been sent to gather data about the ocean's depths. Their ship will be moving in straight rows across the surface of the water.

Part One

Materials: various shoe boxes, blocks of Styrofoam (various shapes and sizes), 5-inch (13 cm) wooden meat skewers, nail or awl, Ocean Bottom Graph for the lid of each box (page 38), seven copies of the Graph for the Ocean Floor Data (page 39) for each group, tape, scissors

Lesson Preparation: Tape the Ocean Bottom Graph to the lid of each shoe box and then use a nail or awl to poke holes through each of the dots on the lid. Place the Styrofoam blocks snugly in the shoe box.

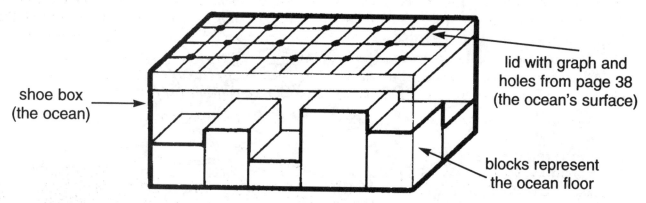

shoe box
(the ocean)

lid with graph and
holes from page 38
(the ocean's surface)

blocks represent
the ocean floor

Mark the length of the meat skewers in centimeters to be used as depth probes. Each group of students will need one depth probe.

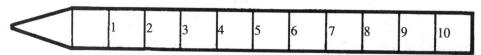

For each group, make a set of seven graphs from page 39. One graph will be used for each horizontal row on the box top (A–G).

Procedure: Distribute a shoe box, depth probe, and seven data graphs to each group. Demonstrate how to use the depth probes by inserting one into the hole which is 1, A on the boxtop graph. Measure how deeply it goes when it strikes the block below. Read the number off the probe, which appears at sea level (top of the box).

Deep as the Ocean *(cont.)*

Procedure *(cont.)*:

Use a transparency of page 39, and mark it as representing Row A and then place a dot at the depth in centimeters just measured for point 1, A. Ask a student volunteer to test for the next depth, 2, A, and mark it on the transparency of the graph. Continue this until you are sure all of the students understand how to graph the depth. Explain that each row, A–G, will have its own graph. Explain that each row on a separate piece of paper.

Tell the students to do this with their group's shoe box ocean, taking turns probing and recording the data. Have the students make a new graph for each of the rows until all seven are finished. Students will finish their graphs by connecting the dots to show the contour of their ocean floors.

━━━━━━━━━━━━━━━━━━━━━━ **Part Two** ━━━━━━━━━━━━━━━━━━━━━━

Materials: all materials from Part One, two thin 6½-inch (17 cm) wooden meat skewers for each group, hole punchers

Lesson Preparation: Mark off the 10-inch (25 cm) skewers with a mark every two centimeters. Label these marks A–G.

Procedure: After the students have completed Part One, ask them to cut their seven data graphs along the data lines they created. Dispose of the bottom portions. Have them punch two holes through the black dots at the top of each graph. Next, tell each group to place their two long skewers between two piles of books. The graphs are going to be threaded onto the skewers, so make sure that the book piles are tall enough that the skewers and graphs will be suspended over the table. The graphs should be placed in the same order as they appear on the lid of the box, beginning with A.

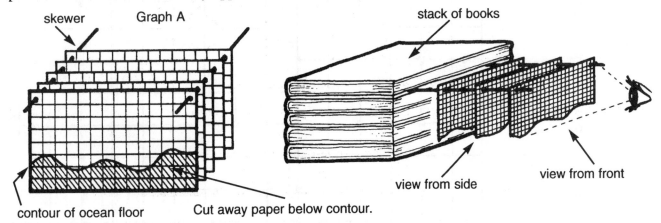

Closure: When data graphs A–G have been suspended from the long skewers and each separated by two centimeters, let the students remove the lid of the box to see the contours of the objects inside. They should match the view of the graphs when they are viewed at table level. The paper represents the water; the empty space below represents the contours of the ocean floor. Explain that today scientists can use a computer to convert this type of data into drawings of the contours of the ocean floor to create maps.

Deep as the Ocean *(cont.)*

Cut out this graph and tape it to the top of a shoe box lid. Using a nail or awl, punch holes through the black dots.

Ocean Bottom Graph

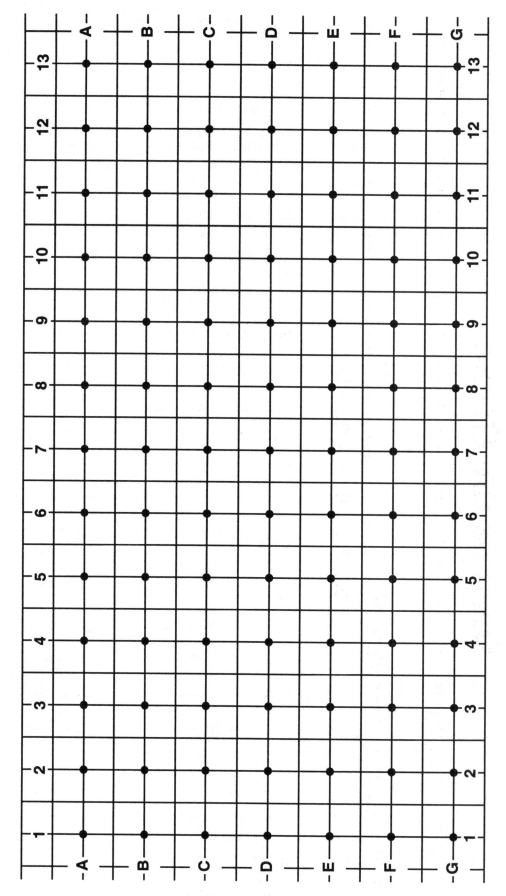

Deep as the Ocean *(cont.)*

Use seven copies of this graph to record data for each row of your shoe box, A–G. Label the graph on the blank in the top left corner. For example, your first graph would be Row A.

Cut along this line before hanging the graph from the skewers.

Graph for Ocean Floor Data

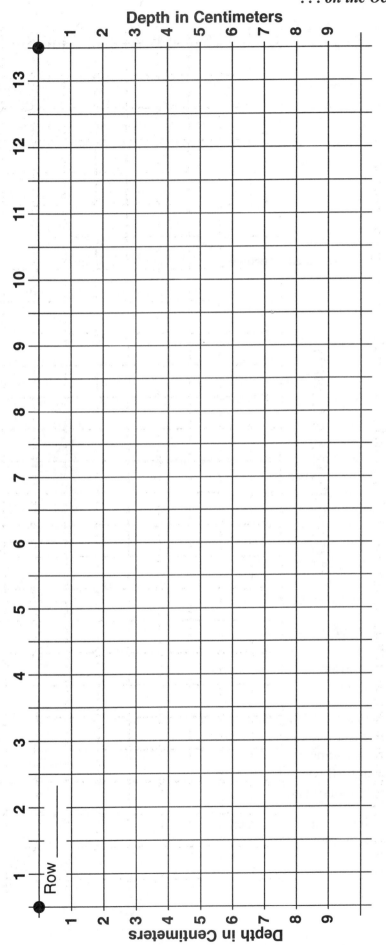

Depth in Centimeters

Row _____

Depth in Centimeters

Constructing a Coral Reef Picture

The magic school bus zooms to the surface and turns into a glass-bottomed boat and sails over a colorful coral reef. Everyone dives overboard for a closer look at the coral and the fish. Amanda Jane's report tells that each tiny "coral polyp grows a stony skeleton around itself." It then attaches itself to other polyps, forming colonies of coral. These take on interesting shapes, sometimes resembling a brain, fan, or horns.

They are brightly colored by algae, and beautiful fish make their home in the coral reefs.

Tim's report tells about the three types of reefs. These are the *fringing reef,* which grows around a land mass; the *barrier reef,* which forms away from a land mass, creating a moat of ocean water; and the *atoll,* which is a coral ring formed around a sunken volcano.

Corals are found where the ocean is warm, in places like the South Pacific, Florida, Australia, East Indies, and southeastern coast of Africa.

A coral reef is an exciting place to go snorkeling. All you need is a face mask, fins, and a snorkel. It is great fun to float face down, just watching the brightly colored fish swimming among the coral. You may even hear the crunching sound of the parrot fish eating algae off the coral. It eats bits of coral in this process, which it cannot digest, so it expels the coral into the water, leaving behind a fine sand.

Try making a pop-up picture of a coral reef.

Materials: two pieces of stiff paper or large file cards, magazine or postcard pictures of coral and sea life found in the reefs or your own pictures, small sharp scissors, glue

Procedure: Cut one piece of stiff paper or large file card to the size you need for your picture and trim the second piece so that it will be about two inches (5 cm) shorter lengthwise and then fold it in half.

Paste a picture of life in a coral reef on the larger stiff paper or use your creativity to make one of your own. You may even want to include the Magic Bus in your picture or a drawing of yourself snorkeling.

Fold the picture card into four equal parts lengthwise so that it forms a staircase. Use the scissors to cut halfway around some of the things in the picture so they will stand out when the staircase is glued or stapled to the shorter card.

Fasten the picture card to the blank card, as shown below, so that it holds it like a staircase.

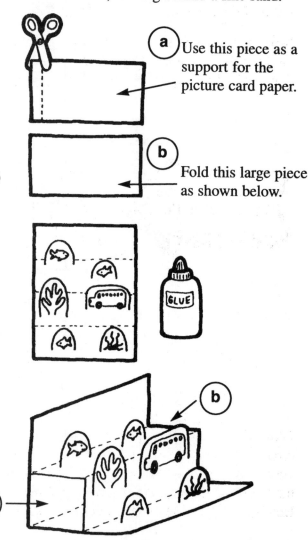

a Use this piece as a support for the picture card paper.

b Fold this large piece as shown below.

Ocean Currents

Next, the bus becomes flat and turns into a giant surfboard. Ms. Frizzle steers the board to shore with all of the passengers on board. They see a school of dolphins leaping nearby and a sperm whale. Phoebe's report tells about the ocean currents. Ocean currents are caused by temperatures and the amount of salt in the water. Currents, which were explored earlier in the water density experiments, flow from the surface to the bottom and then back again. Ocean currents caused by winds sweep in great swirls in a horizontal motion due to the spinning of the earth around its axis. Do an experiment to see how this works.

Materials: large globe, blue felt pen with washable ink

Lesson Preparation: Test the washable ink on a small part of the globe to be sure that you will be able to wash it off after this activity. If it does not wash off with water, the ink is not a washable pen so replace it with another and test it to be sure it will wash off.

Procedure: Place the globe on a table. Begin to rotate it so that it turns west to east, just as the real earth turns. Put the point of the pen near the North Pole and draw a straight line from the pole to the equator as the globe spins. Press the pen lightly on the globe so it does not stop spinning. Lift the pen and return to the pole again for another downward stroke. Repeat this about ten times and then stop the globe and look at the marks. Use the picture of the globe below to show how the pen marks look north of the equator.

Next, do this same experiment for the Southern Hemisphere. Rotate the globe in the same direction but have the pen stokes begin at the South Pole and go up to the equator. Draw what these lines look like south of the equator on the globe. Compare the marks; are they the same?

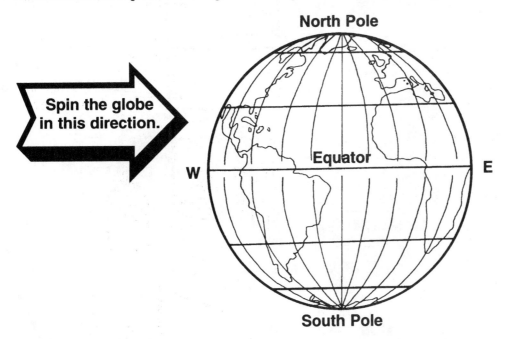

Closure: The spinning of the earth from west to east causes the winds to move in the opposite direction, east to west. The winds blow across the ocean water and create currents which move in a westerly direction. The water is deflected (turned aside) by the continents. This causes ocean water in the Northern Hemisphere to move clockwise (the way the clock hands turn) and in the Southern Hemisphere to move counterclockwise (the opposite direction of clock hands).

Ocean Currents *(cont.)*

Sailors, even before Columbus, learned that they could ride great distances on the ocean currents. Look at the map of the Ocean Currents and the map of the Voyages of Columbus on page 43 and then answer the questions about these maps on page 44.

A—Japan Current
B—North Equatorial Current
C—Equatorial Counter Current
D—South Equatorial Current
E—Humboldt Current

F—West Wind Drift
G—Gulf Stream
H—North Atlantic Drift
I—Canaries
J—Guinea Current

K—Brazil Current
L—Benguela Current
M—Agulhas Current
N—West Australian Current
O—East Australian Current

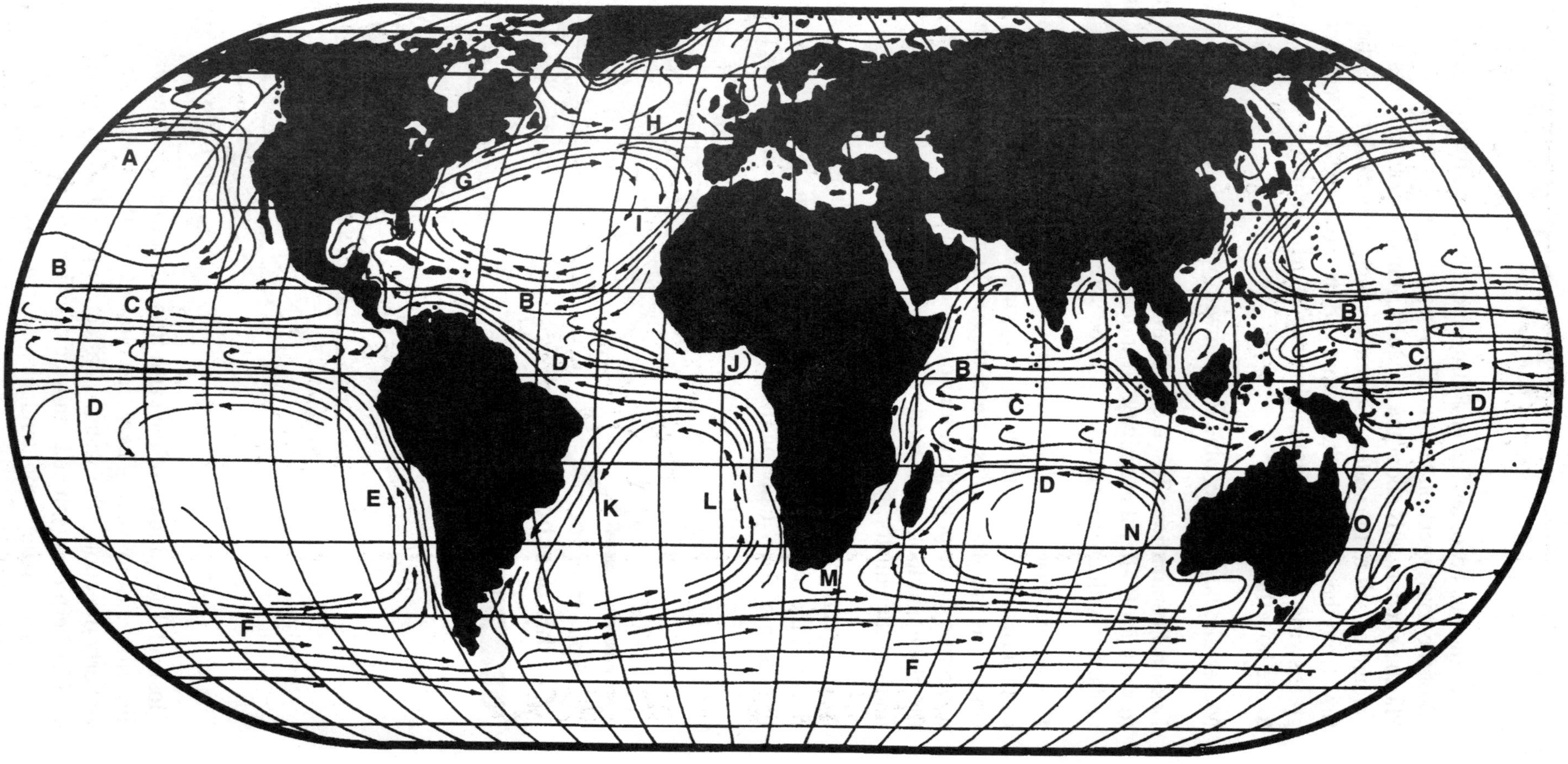

Ocean Currents *(cont.)*

Voyages of Columbus

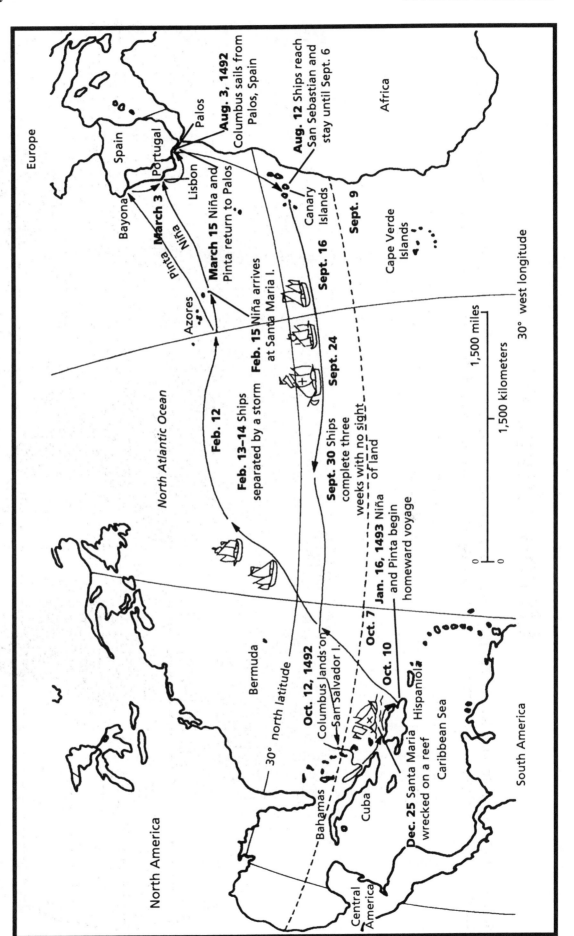

Ocean Currents *(cont.)*

You will need a dictionary, a map of the world which has names of countries on it, and the maps shown on pages 42 and 43 to answer the following questions.

1. Compare the maps of the ocean currents and Columbus' voyages on pages 42 and 43 and then write an explanation for how his ships could sail from Palos, Spain, by going south and then west. Tell why Columbus' ships returned to Portugal along a different route.

   _____

   _____

   _____

   _____

2. If you wanted to sail from Seattle, Washington, to the Hawaiian Islands, what directions would you sail and on which currents?

   _____

   _____

   _____

   _____

3. Sailors called the water near the equator the *doldrums*. Look up this word in a dictionary and then write what it means. Tell why the sailors feared going into this area.

   _____

   _____

   _____

4. Find the only ocean current which travels all around the world. (**Hint**: It is in the Southern Hemisphere.)

   _____

   _____

   _____

5. Some scientists believe that Leif Ericson, a Norse explorer, may have been the first non-North American person to reach North America, arriving in the year 1,000 A.D. Stories from that time tell of his sailing to a land west of Greenland, where he lived at the time. The ruins of an old Norse settlement were discovered in 1960 in Newfoundland.

Look at the map and see if you can find a possible route this early explorer may have used to sail from Greenland to Newfoundland and back again. Draw a picture of this route on the back of this paper and label the ocean currents.

What Did You Learn?

To the Teacher: This unit assessment is an open-ended question which lets students apply the knowledge they gleaned during this study, as well as their creativity. Establish a rubric which will award points for accuracy, effort, and originality.

To the Student: You have just finished traveling aboard the magic school bus through the continental shelf and slope, deep ocean floor, and the coral reefs. Now, use what you have learned and your imagination to turn yourself into a real sea animal which lives in the ocean. Describe the animal you have become and explain where you live and how your body has adapted to the temperature, currents, amount of light, pressure, and other conditions in this area. Give details of how you move, what you eat, and how you defend yourself. (Use the back of this page or a separate piece of paper, if you need more room.)

_____

_____

_____

_____

_____

_____

_____

_____

_____

_____

_____

_____

_____

_____

After describing the animal you have become, make a drawing of this animal on a separate piece of paper. Add labels to point out the details of your drawing. Color your drawing to make it complete.

Related Books and Materials

Center for Marine Conservation. *The Ocean Book.* (Center for Marine Conservation, 1989.) Order from the National Science Teachers Association (800) 722-NSTA. This activity book on the world of oceans and the living things that inhabit them is filled with experiments, investigations, puzzles, and games. The activities were created and contributed by leading aquatic centers.

Chovan, Judith and Sara Crump. *Sharks: Fact and Fantasy.* (Natural History Museum of Los Angeles County, 1990.) This colorful, fact-filled book is an outstanding reference for the study of sharks. Order from the Education Division of the Natural History Museum (213) 744-3466.

Cole, Joanna. *The Magic School Bus® On the Ocean Floor.* (Scholastic, 1992.)

Lemonick, Michael D. "The Last Frontier." (*Time Magazine*, August 14, 1995.) This article gives recent information about probing the abyss of the ocean, and it includes a graphic description of equipment used to dive to various depths.

"Oceans." (*Kids Discover,* February 1992.) This outstanding and colorful issue has easy-to-read information about the ocean. Order back issues from Kids Discover, 170 Fifth Ave., 6th Floor, NY, NY 10010, (212) 242-5133.

Thurman, Harold. *Essentials of Oceanography.* (Merrill, 1990.) An extensive coverage of oceanography, this book includes topics of the history of oceanography, origin of the oceans, circulation, waves, and tides.

Wade, Larry. *Getting to Know Whales.* (1995.) Order from the National Science Teachers Association (800) 722-NSTA. A book for young scientists who want to study whales, its activities are based on data supplied by whale biologists.

Wade, Larry. *Oceanography: Whales in the Classroom.* (1992.) Order from the National Science Teachers Association (800) 722-NSTA. This fascinating book offers a broad introduction to many aspects of oceanography, including the geology of sea floors, biology of ocean life, and currents.

Wexo, John Bonnett. *Sharks.* (Zoobooks, 1988.) This outstanding book covers the history, anatomy, and interesting facts about sharks. Order from Wildlife Education, Ltd., 3590 Kettner Blvd., San Diego, CA 92101.

Young, Ruth. *Science/Literature Unit: The Magic School Bus® Inside the Earth.* (Teacher Created Materials, Inc. 1996.) This book offers science activities to extend the popular book *The Magic School Bus® Inside the Earth* by Joanna Cole. Topics include the earth's interior and moving crust.

The Magic School Bus® Explores the Ocean. Software. Microsoft. 800-426-0856. Ms. Frizzle and her students ride the magic school bus into the ocean. This program is filled with games and experiments based on the ocean theme.

National Geographic Society. P.O. Box 2118, Washington, D.C. 20013-2118, (800) 447-0647. Order a back-to-back map of the floors of the Indian and Pacific Oceans, including information on deep vents, catalog #02742. A video of *Sharks, #50501, Realms of the Sea*, a fully illustrated book, and *Seasons in the Sea*, a video, #80580, may also be orderd.

National Science Teachers Association. (800) 722-NSTA. Order the 60 in. x 40 in. (150 cm x 100 cm) "The Dynamic Planet" poster. This poster of Earth's volcanoes, earthquake epicenters, and outline of the tectonic plates was done by the U.S. Geological Survey and the Smithsonian Institution. Also order the *Jason IV: Baja California Sur* curriculum, which contains extensive activities related to deep sea vents, whales, and ocean exploration.

Pangea Digital Pictures. 212 Tucker St., Healdsbrug, CA 95448-4423, (800) 663-2319. Order the 40-minute *Oceanography* video, narrated by oceanographer Dr. Sylvia Earle.

Tidelines, Inc. P.O. Box 431, Encinitas, CA 92024, (800) 345-8542. Order the calendar of the tides for any of 22 locations on the east and west coasts of the U.S. and two areas of Australia. The calendars show a daily tide graph for each month of the year.

Answer Key

Page 8 (How Big Is the Ocean?)

1. 10°

3. 9 latitude sections

4. 36 longitude sections. The answer can be arrived at by counting the longitude sections in one ring of latitude or by arithmetic, $360° \div 10° = 36$ longitude sections.

5. 9 latitude sections x 36 longitude sections = 324 total sections on one map

6. 324 total sections on one map x 2 = 648 total sections on both maps

The amount of the earth covered by ocean is shown on the chart below.

This method of measuring the amount of ocean covering the earth is not exact and thus does not match the amount given by scientists which is nearly 71%.

Amount of the Earth Covered by Water

Latitude Section	Northern Hemisphere	Southern Hemisphere
0° - 10°	30 sections	26 sections
10° - 20°	28 sections	28 sections
20° - 30°	22 sections	28 sections
30° - 40°	19 sections	33 sections
40° - 50°	15 sections	35 sections
50° - 60°	14 sections	35 sections
60° - 70°	8 sections	36 sections
70° - 80°	29 sections	12 sections
80° - 90°	34 sections	3 sections
Totals:	199 (N) sections	236 (S) sections

199 (N) + 236 (S) = 435 (T) Total sections covered by oceans

435 (T) ÷ 648 (MT)* = 67* % of earth covered by oceans

*Student answers will vary but should be between 60% and 70%

Page 11 (Gone Fishing)

Fish use their tail fins (caudal) to push them through the water, just as we use our feet. The fins on their sides (pectoral) are used like our arms and are used to pull them through the water.

The drawings students make should show details of the locations and shapes of the fins, gills, eyes, and mouth. Labels should be simple and need not include the names of the fins at this point.

Page 12 (Comparing Saltwater to Freshwater)

1. The saltwater sinks to the bottom of the cup of freshwater.

2. The freshwater drops float on the top of the saltwater.

3. The waters do not balance each other. They have different densities; the saltwater is heavier than the freshwater.

4. When freshwater flows into saltwater, it floats on the surface for some distance until they mix.

Page 13 (Comparing Warm to Cold Water)

1. The cold water sinks in the room temperature water. (Cold water has a greater density.)

1. The hot water stays on the top.

3. Cold water in the areas near the Arctic and Antarctic plunges beneath the warmer waters.

Page 16 (What Causes the Tides?)

1. No.

2. 2, 3, 4, 5, and 16, 17, 18 should be circled.

3. 10, 11, 12, and 24, 25, 26 should be circled.

5. The dates of the full moon (February 4) and new moon (February 18) coincide with the highest and lowest of the tides. The dates of the moderate tides coincide with the dates of the last quarter (February 12) and first quarter (February 25). This evidence supports the fact that the moon's phases cause the tides as it orbits the earth. (For further information, see the Explanation of the Tides on pages 19 and 20 and the February 1996, Tide Calendar on page 48.)

Page 44 (Ocean Currents)

1. Columbus sailed on the Canaries Current which carried his ships south and then west across the Atlantic Ocean. On his return trip, he followed the Gulf Stream north and then east.

2. You would sail south on the Japan Current and then west on the North Equatorial Currents to reach the Hawaiian Islands from Seattle, WA.

3. The doldrums are areas where winds die down and ships cannot sail. When ships depended upon sails for energy, this meant a slow death without fresh water if they could not get out of the doldrums.

4. The West Wind Drift is the current which travels around the world below the continents in the Southern Hemisphere.

5. Leif Ericson most likely used the North Atlantic Drift to carry his ship to and from Greenland.

Answer Key *(cont.)*

The chart below represents the final result of the activity on pages 14-18 (What Causes the Tides?). Each student's chart may be corrected by referring to his/her individual date below.

February 1996

Tide Calendar

. . . *on the Ocean Floor*

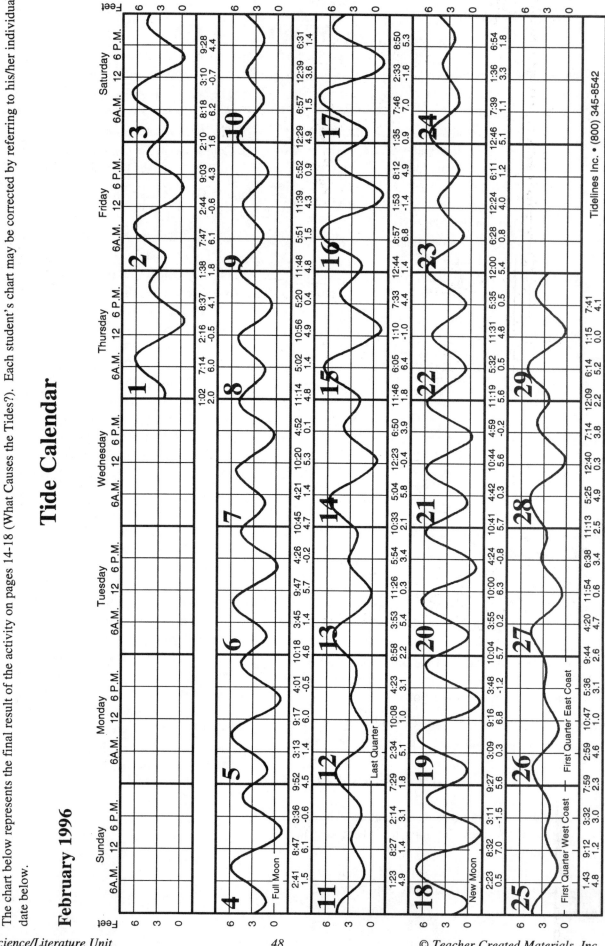